Fall For *Jesus* He Never Leaves

ASHLEY WILLIAMS

AuthorHouse™
1663 Liberty Drive
Bloomington, IN 47403
www.authorhouse.com
Phone: 833-262-8899

Because of the dynamic nature of the Internet, any web addresses or links contained in this book may have changed since publication and may no longer be valid. The views expressed in this work are solely those of the author and do not necessarily reflect the views of the publisher, and the publisher hereby disclaims any responsibility for them.

Any people depicted in stock imagery provided by Getty Images are models, and such images are being used for illustrative purposes only.
Certain stock imagery © Getty Images.

This book is printed on acid-free paper.

ISBN: 979-8-8230-1975-0 (sc)
ISBN: 979-8-8230-1976-7 (e)

Library of Congress Control Number: 2023924367

Print information available on the last page.

Published by AuthorHouse 02/02/2023

authorHOUSE®

Dedication

This book is dedicated to God, God brought me through so much, and I had an epiphany that the hand of God was on my life, I want to thank God for saving my life, and guiding me on my spiritual walk with him. My bond/ relationship with God is indissoluble and I love it, and this is where my life is complete because only God can fill that void. I want the whole world to know God can save their life too, hallelujah, and praise God. Ashley Williams. :)

1/30/21

For a day in thy courts is better than thousand I rather be a doorkeeper in the house of my God, than to dwell in the tents of wickedness.

Psalms 84:10

1/31/22

Yea doubtless, and I count all things but loss for the excellency of the knowledge of Christ Jesus my Lord; for whom I have suffered the loss of all things, and do count them but dung, that I may win Christ.

Philippians 3:8

2/2/22

The law of the Lord is perfect, converting the soul: the testimony of the Lord is sure, making wise the simple.
Psalms 19:7

11/27/22

These words spake Jesus, and lifted up his eyes to heaven, and said, Father, the hour is come; glorify my Son, that thy Son also may glorify thee; John 17:1

Trust in him at all times, ye people, pour out your heart before him: God is a refuge for us. Psalms 62:8

12/9/22

The Church is within Me

Many spend a lifetime seeking riches, fortune and fame forsaking friends, family and loved ones, what a shame! We should've learned but read what is love your neighbor as yourself," while waiting in line, be kind, patient, and, cool, these are the things we should have learned in Sunday School.

12/9/2022

Jesus Christ was Crucified

As the bible stated, "For God so loved the world, that He gave His only begotten Son, that whosoever believeth in him should not perish, but have everlasting life." All praises to God! ☺

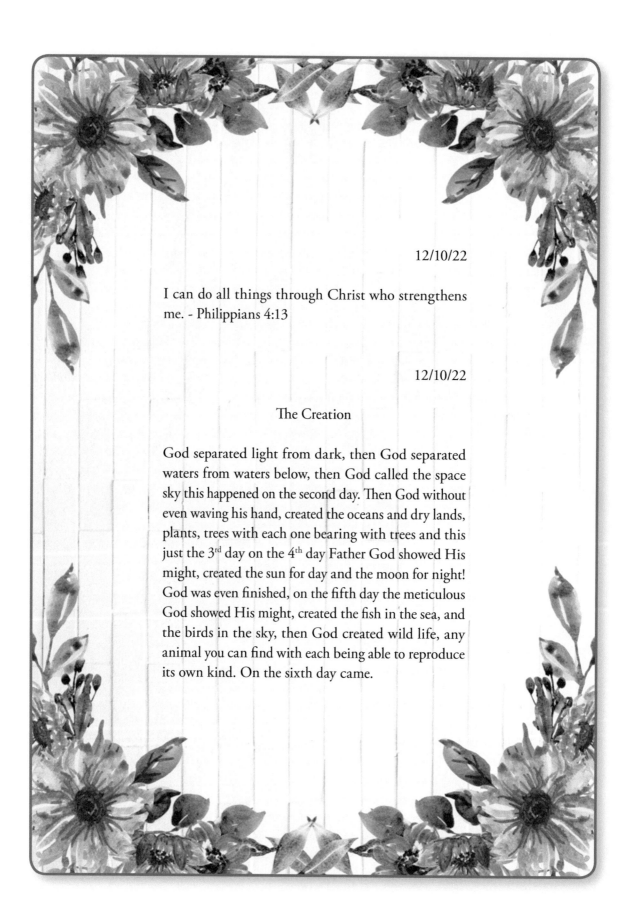

12/10/22

I can do all things through Christ who strengthens me. - Philippians 4:13

12/10/22

The Creation

God separated light from dark, then God separated waters from waters below, then God called the space sky this happened on the second day. Then God without even waving his hand, created the oceans and dry lands, plants, trees with each one bearing with trees and this just the 3rd day on the 4th day Father God showed His might, created the sun for day and the moon for night! God was even finished, on the fifth day the meticulous God showed His might, created the fish in the sea, and the birds in the sky, then God created wild life, any animal you can find with each being able to reproduce its own kind. On the sixth day came.

12/11/22

A very astronomical plan God said, "Let us make man, man was created from the dust of the ground. God breathed into his nostrils, and man became a living soul."

12/12/22

Due to the disobidence through 1776-1985 African Americans were enslaved children being sold as slaves.

12/12/22

Adam and Eve

When the making of all the animals was done. God brought them to Adam to name each one. Animals are creatures not to abandon, but Adam himself needed a companion to keep, Adam awoke and was pleased with God's plan, Adam said, "She's part of me and called her woman from the tree of knowledge, Adam and Eve were not to eat, but the serpent was shrewd, and full of deceit. The serpent then called God a lie, told Eve, "you shall not surely die" the serpent said, "God knows it will open your eyes, and you will be like God, all knowing and wise." So the woman went ahead and did eat some, then Adam ate, after she gave him one, their eyes opened they knew nakedness and shame, since then things have never been the same yet God never left his people this is when disobedience came into play by their actions and God's wrath were upon them.

12/13/2022

Parted the Red Sea

As the bible stated, "God ordered Moses to stretch out his staff over the Red Sea, and the Red Sea parted. This allowed the Israelites to escape across the sea, and away from Egypt unharmed in the 13th century BCE."

12/13/22

"For we walk by faith not by sight"
- 2 Corinthians 5:7

"For God gave us a spirit not of fear but of power and love and self control."
2 Timothy 1:7

Faith can move mountains
Matthew 17:20

12/16/22

God was ready to destroy people & earth because the world was full of violence.

As the bible stated, "So God said to Noah, "I am going to put and end to all people, for earth is filled with violence because of them, I am surely going to destroy both them and the earth.

12/22/22

God is a Healer

As the bible said, "God heals the brokenhearted and bandages their wounds," the good news no matter how heartbroken you're! I can admit I'm a living testimony because God healed me, all praises to God! ☺

Fall for Jesus he never leaves

12/23/22

Train up a child where its should go, and when he is old he won't depart

Every parents should teach their children about God, this is what we should've learned in Sunday School. As the bible stated, "Train up a child in the way he should go; and when he is old, he will not depart from it."

12/24/22

We're Oneness with God

We should always love one another treating one another with the upmost respect as we want to be treated! That is what make God happy! Kindness is the new cool! ☺

12/25/22

I'm ambiguous if people think they came into the world by their parents alone that is very selfish thinking when it's stated in the bible "You knit me together in my mothers womb," we should always give credit where its due to God! Without God we wouldn't exist! Accept Jesus as your personal savior, after all God sacrificed his son for us, he proved his love and loyalty to us all. That is loyalty that no other family member, friend, spouse, bff, etc have ever done for us because God will never leave.

12/25/22

Oneness with God

It doesn't matter what background you came from, rather your guardians believed in God, it's your responsibility to know God on a intiminate level pray your spirit will lead you where its suppose to be at with one with God, because that is the only way to make it in this world God must be involved in your life!

I will praise thee, for I am peacefully and wonderfully made marvellous are thy words; and that my soul knoweth right well. Psalms 139:14

Make a joyful noise unto the Lord, all ye lands Psalms 100:1

I lift up my eyes to the mountains - where does my help come from? My help comes from the Lord, the maker of heaven and earth Psalm 121:1-2

1/7/23

There is that speaketh like the piercings of a sword, but the tongue of the wise is health. Proverbs 12:18

Trust in the Lord, and do good; so shalt thou dwell in the land, and verily thou shalt be fed.

Psalms 37:3

1/27/23

But ye, brethren, be not weary in well doing.

2 Thessalonians 3:13

1/29/23

For John truly baptized with water: but
ye shall be baptized with the Holy Ghost
not many days hence.

Acts 1:5

1/29/23

For John truly baptized with water: but
ye shall be baptized with the Holy Ghost
not many days hence.

Acts 1:5

2/7/23

His will His way my faith

Jeremiah 29:11

12/13/23

God has forgiven all your mistakes

Psalm 103:12

Let your light shine

Matthew 5:4

Let nothing be done through strife or vainglory, but in lowliness of mind yet each esteem other better than themselves

Philippians 2:3

The grace of the Lord Jesus Christ, and the love of God, and the communion of the Holy Ghost, be with you all. Amen

2 Corinthians

I pray not that thou shouldest take them out of the world, but that thou shouldest keep them from evil John 17:15

I delight to do my will O my God, yea, thy law is within my heart Psalms 40:1

Looking for that blessed hope, and the glorious appearing of the great God and our Saviour Jesus Christ;
Titus 2:13

For the earth shall be filled with the knowledge of the glory of the Lord, as the waters cover sea.
Habakkuk 2:14

Help us, O God for our salvation, for the glory of thy name: and deliver us, and purge away our sins, for thy names sake..
Psalms 79:9

He has made everything
Beautiful
in its time.
Ecclesiastes 3:11

he hears us

1 john 5:14

Get ready, get ready!
Jesus is coming soon!

Do not be
anxious about
anything, but in every
situation, by prayer
and petition, with
thanksgiving, present
your requests to God.

And the peace of
God, which transcends
all understanding, will
guard your hearts
and your minds in
Christ Jesus.

Philippians 4:6-7

GOD
WILL
PROVIDE
PHILIPPIANS 4:19

He heals
THE WOUNDS
OF EVERY
Shattered
HEART
PSALM 147:3

Don't you know
that you yourselves
are God's temple
and that God's
Spirit dwells in your
midst?
1 Corinthians 3:16

Trust
IN THE LORD WITH ALL YOUR
Heart
AND LEAN NOT ON YOUR OWN
understanding
PROV 3:5

Thy testimonies are very: holiness becometh thine house, O Lord, for ever

Delight
Yourself also in
the **Lord** and
He shall give you
the *desires* of
your heart.
Psalm 37:4

Trust
IN THE LORD
WITH ALL YOUR HEART
AND LEAN NOT ON YOUR
OWN UNDERSTANDING;
IN ALL YOUR WAYS
SUBMIT TO HIM,
AND HE WILL MAKE
your paths straight
PROVERBS 3:5-6

"This is the day
that the Lord acted;
we will rejoice and
celebrate in it!"

PSALM 118:24

Be strong
and courageous

JOSHUA 1:9

*"Do not grieve, for
the joy of the Lord
is your strength."*

-Nehemiah 8:10

For God so loved the world,
that he gave his only begotten
Son; that whosoever believeth
in him should not perish,
but have everlasting life.
John 3:16

Night Prayer

For God so loved the world, that he gave his only begotten Son, that
whosoever believeth in him should not perish, but have everlasting life.
For God sent not his Son into the world to condemn the world; but that
the world through him might be saved.

John 1:1 KJV
In the beginning was the
Word, and the Word was
with God, and the Word
was God.

"Come to Me,
all you who
labor and are
heavy laden,
and I will
give you rest."
Matthew 11:28

LOVE THE LORD
YOUR GOD WITH ALL YOUR HEART
WITH ALL YOUR SOUL & WITH ALL YOUR MIND
WITH ALL Y OUR
STRENGTH

This is the day
that the Lord has made;
Let us rejoice
and be glad in it.

Psalm 118:24

Strength and honour
are her clothing;
and she shall rejoice
in time to come.
Proverbs 31:25

God is my
strength and power.

The Lord himself goes
before you and will be
with you; he will never
leave you nor forsake
you. Do not be afraid;
do not be discouraged.

THE
Lord WILL
FIGHT FOR YOU;
YOU NEED ONLY TO
Be Still.
EXODUS 14:14

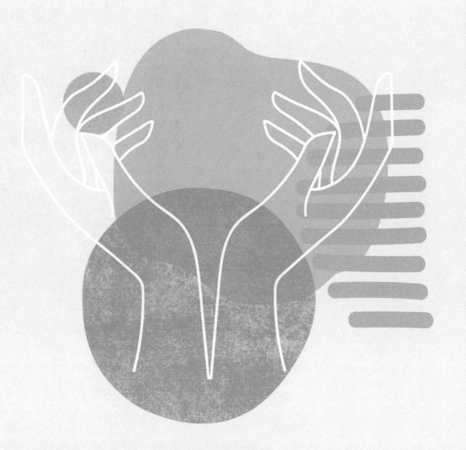

The Lord himself
goes before you
and will be with you;
but will never leave you
nor forsake you.
Do not be afraid,
Do not be discouraged.

JOHN 8:12 (NIV)

I am the light of the world. Whoever follows me will never walk in darkness. But will have the light of life.

John 1:1 KJV

In the beginning was the Word, and the Word was with God, and the Word was God.

Jesus is not only my God

He is my friend ♥

Printed in the United States
by Baker & Taylor Publisher Services